AF605698

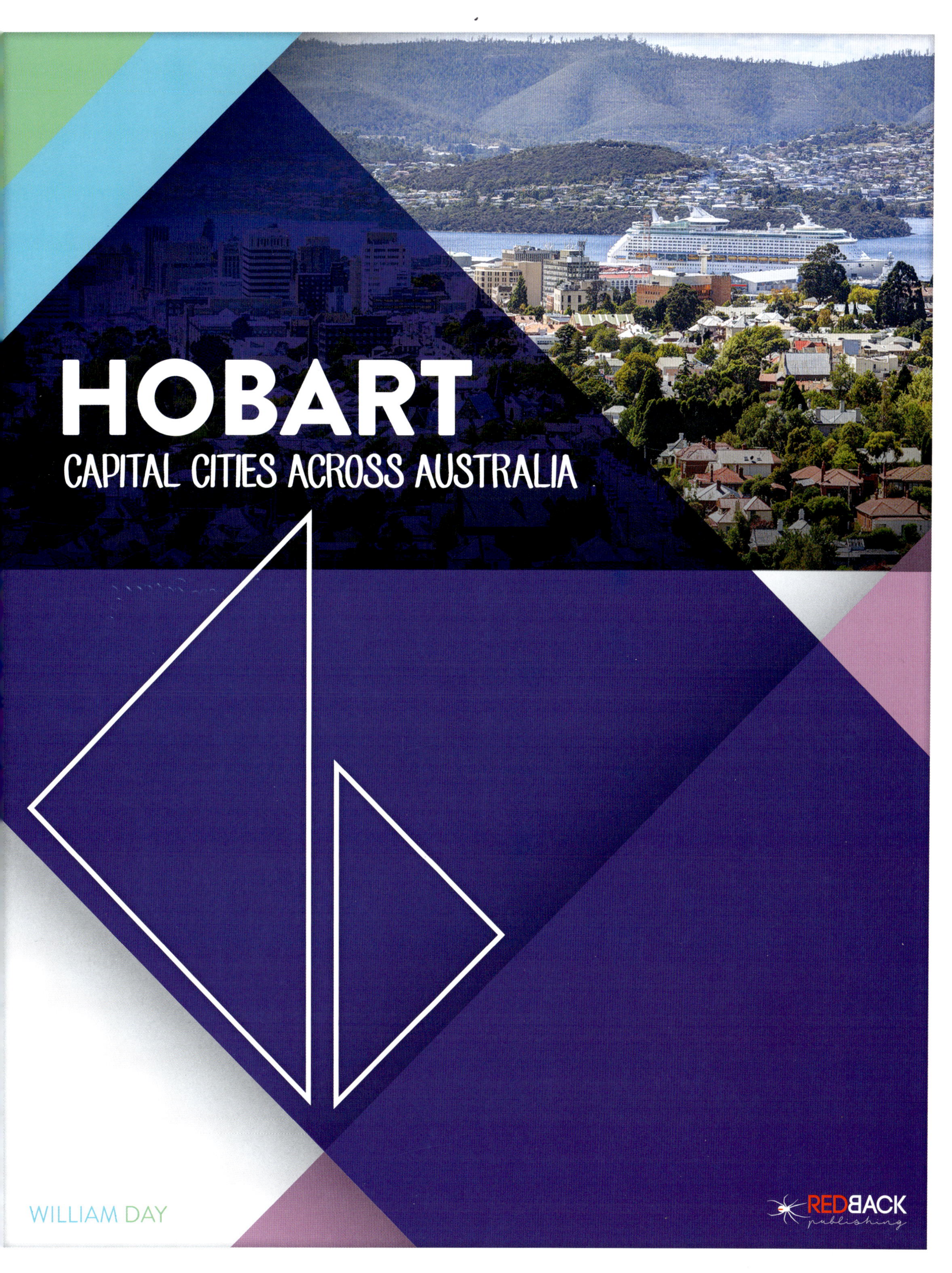
HOBART
CAPITAL CITIES ACROSS AUSTRALIA
WILLIAM DAY
REDBACK publishing

Redback Publishing
PO Box 357 Frenchs Forest NSW 2086
Australia

www.redbackpublishing.com.au
orders@redbackpublishing.com.au

978-1-925860-50-4

Author: William Day
Editor: Marianne Lindsell
Designer: Redback Publishing

Original illustrations © Redback Publishing 2019
Originated by Redback Publishing

Printed and bound in China by Leo Paper

Acknowledgements
Abbreviations: l—left, r—right, b—bottom, t—top, c—centre, m—middle
We would like to thank the following for permission to reproduce photographs: (Images © shutterstock) p6b Recherche and Espérance-François Roux mg 0574, François Geoffroi Roux [Public domain], via Wikimedia commons, p8t 1837 Dower Map of Van Dieman's Land or Tasmania - Geographicus - Tazmania-dower-1837, http://www.geographicus.com/mm5/cartographers/dower.txt [Public domain], via Wikimedia commons, p9b Hobart Town chain gang, HOBART TOWN CHAIN GANG[1], 1926 [Public domain], via Wikimedia commons, p11 Hobart Mercury building, Nick-D [CC BY-SA 3.0 (https://creativecommons.org/licenses/by-sa/3.0)], via Wikimedia commons, p13t - Flock of Little Pied Cormorants, by KeresH [CC BY-SA 3.0 (https://creativecommons.org/licenses/by-sa/3.0)], via Wikimedia, p16t Dr. Mawson's sledge, by Wellcome Images CC BY 4.0 (https://creativecommons.org/licenses/by/4.0)], via Wikimedia commons, p23t - Hobart Town Hall by Tasmanian Archive and Heritage Office via Wikimedia, p19t Eastern Pygmy Possum , by Photo by Phil Spark [CC BY 2.0 (https://creativecommons.org/licenses/by/2.0)], via Wikimedia commons, p20 The ship Mountstuart Elphinstone offshore by William Adolphus Knell in 1840, William Adolphus Knell [Public domain], via Wikimedia commons, p21 Royal Hobart Hospital, by Annette Teng [CC BY 3.0 (https://creativecommons.org/licenses/by/3.0)], via Wikimedia commons, p23t Town Hall Hobart - Tram in Macquarie Street, by Tasmanian Archives and Heritage Office, [Public Domain], p24b - Pipeline power station Waddamana ca 1900, State Library Victoria, p25t - Group of Women Descending Mt Wellington in a Horse-Drawn Carriage, Mount Wellington, Tasmania, 24 Dec 1912, Museums Victoria Collections [Public Domain], p29t - Photograph - Female Factory, Cascades NS1013/1/1453, Libraries Tasmania, p29b Arthurs Circle in Battery Point, by denisbin, Attribution-NoDerivs 2.0 Generic (CC BY-ND 2.0), via flickr.

Every effort has been made to contact copyright holders of any material reproduced in this book. Any omissions will be rectified in subsequent printings if notice is given to the publisher.

A catalogue record for this book is available from the National Library of Australia

CONTENTS

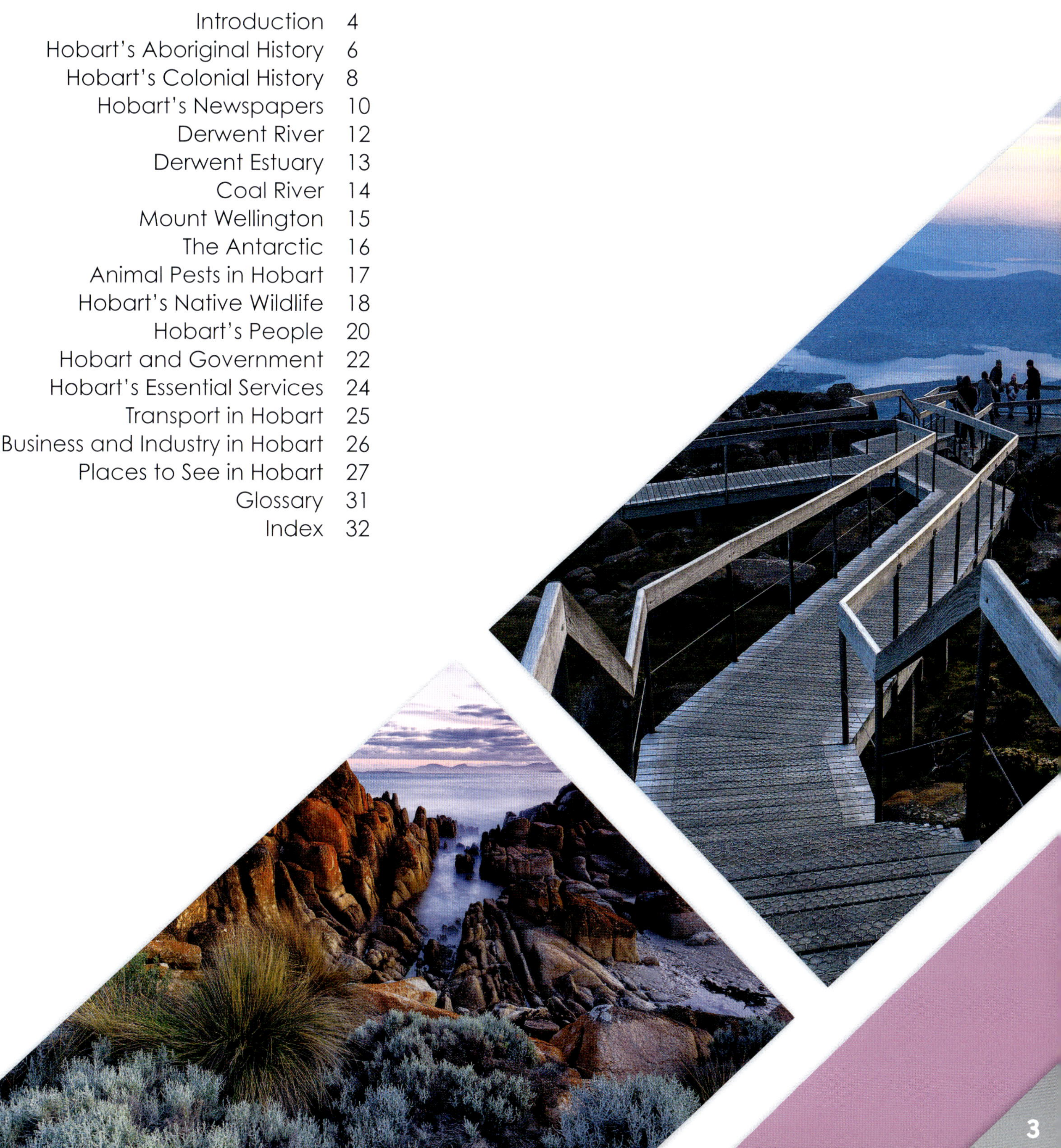

INTRODUCTION

Hobart is the capital city of the Australian state of Tasmania, and is located on the southeast coast of the island.

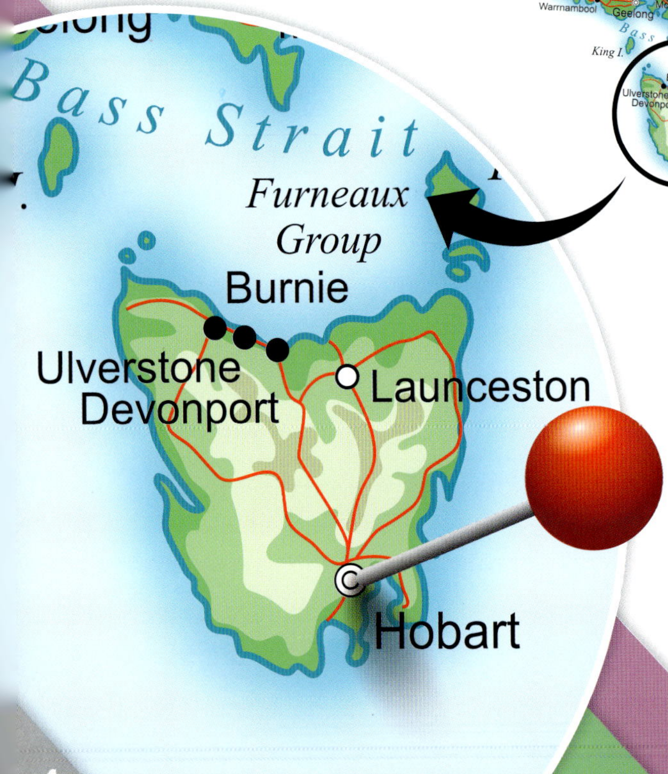

When people refer to Hobart they could mean any one of five different areas

1. The city centre
2. The city centre plus its surrounding suburbs
3. The GCCSA
4. The local government area only
5. A personal idea of where they think the city is

Climate

The ocean currents that surround Tasmania affect Hobart's temperate climate. Being the nearest capital city in Australia to the Antarctic, Hobart is comparatively cold and snow may fall in the winter.

Geology

Hobart is located on the higher regions of an ancient landscape that was flooded when sea levels rose following the end of the last Ice Age, about 10,000 years ago.

Mount Wellington was formed many millions of years ago when molten magma came to the surface, cooled and then hardened. The rock which formed both Mount Wellington and other parts of Hobart in this way is called dolerite.

HOBART FACTS & FIGURES

Population of Greater Hobart in 2017 – 224,500 people

Height above sea level – from 0 metres at sea level to 1,271 metres at Mount Wellington

Area of Greater Hobart – 1,695 square kilometres

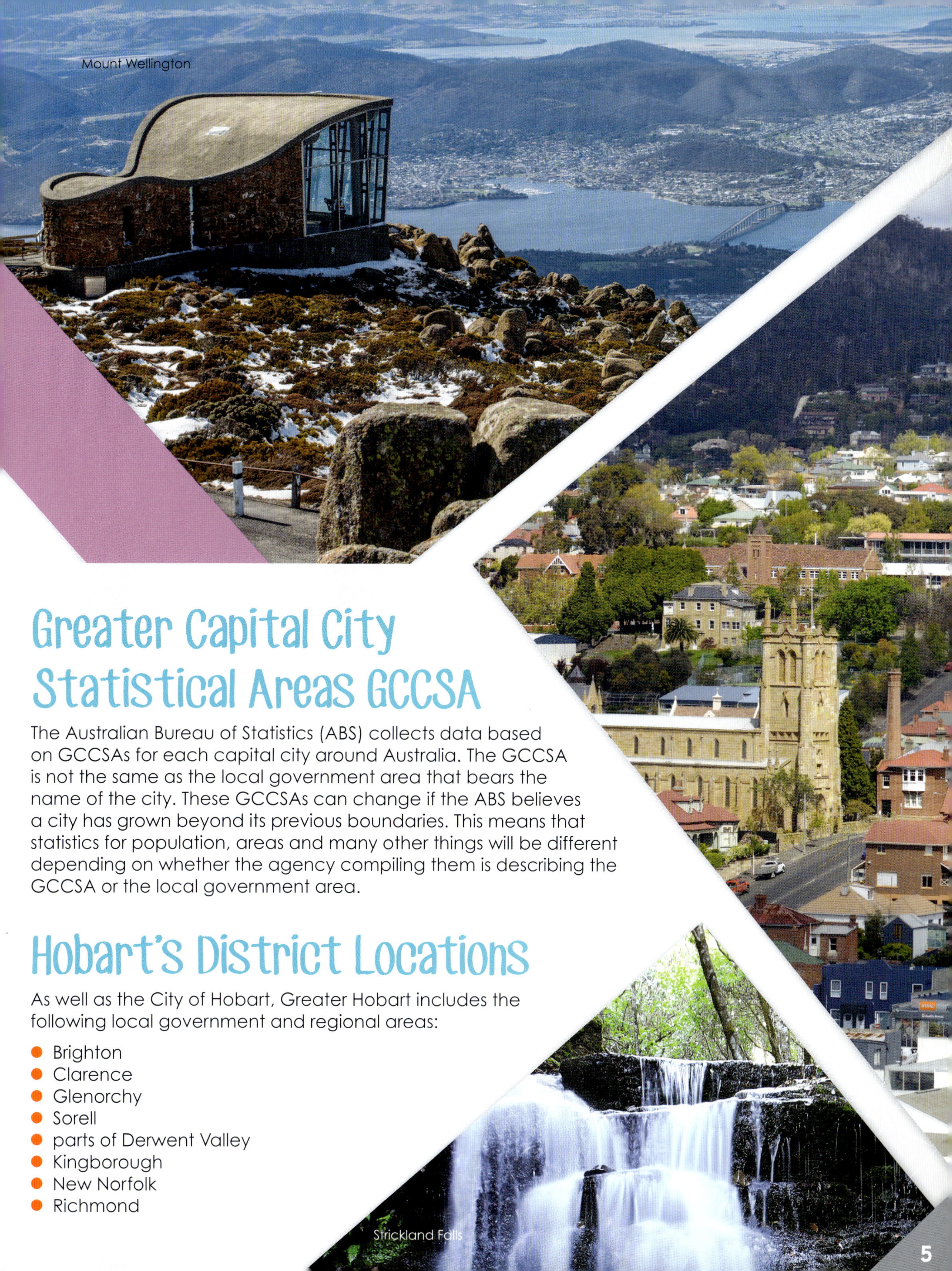

Mount Wellington

Greater Capital City Statistical Areas GCCSA

The Australian Bureau of Statistics (ABS) collects data based on GCCSAs for each capital city around Australia. The GCCSA is not the same as the local government area that bears the name of the city. These GCCSAs can change if the ABS believes a city has grown beyond its previous boundaries. This means that statistics for population, areas and many other things will be different depending on whether the agency compiling them is describing the GCCSA or the local government area.

Hobart's District Locations

As well as the City of Hobart, Greater Hobart includes the following local government and regional areas:

- Brighton
- Clarence
- Glenorchy
- Sorell
- parts of Derwent Valley
- Kingborough
- New Norfolk
- Richmond

Strickland Falls

HOBART'S ABORIGINAL HISTORY

The Aboriginal people of Tasmania, and of Hobart, have an ancestry that dates back to at least 40,000 years ago. They reached Tasmania when it was still joined to the rest of Australia by dry land. At the end of the last Ice Age, about 10,000 years ago, the world's sea levels rose, isolating the people in Tasmania.

When they first arrived in Tasmania, their community was probably the most southerly group of human beings living anywhere in the world. The challenges they faced during the cold winters led them to develop many skills that allowed them to survive.

Secret Falls, Hobart

The First Aboriginal Explorers

Some historians believe the reed canoes that were used by the Tasmanian Aboriginal people may be examples of an extremely ancient technology. They could even be the style of vessels used thousands of years ago when people first began exploring the world and first travelled to the Australian continent. This great exploration occurred a very long time before the 1600s, when European explorers started sailing southwards in journeys that created the Age of Exploration.

European explorers approaching the Derwent River, 1793

The Black War

From the 1820s, a state of war existed between the colonists and the Tasmanian Aboriginal people. The many violent clashes became known as the Black War. In 1830, the colonists formed the Black Line, a group of men who made their way across Tasmania, driving all the remaining Aboriginal people towards the southeast. The idea was to exile all the Tasmanian Aboriginal people to a small area where they would be completely separated from the settlers.

Truganini

Palawa

The Palawa are descendants of the first Australian Aboriginal people of Tasmania. Other groups of descendants have also formed to represent different peoples.

Truganini 1812-1876

Often mistakenly referred to as the last of the Tasmanian Aboriginal people, Truganini suffered at the hands of the colonists, but rose above her own distress to be a guiding influence for her people. She lived through the dark times when Aboriginal people were systematically removed from farming lands, with those still surviving being exiled to small islands. Truganini died in Hobart in 1876. Her remains did not receive a traditional burial until one hundred years later, in1976.

Muwinina

The Muwinina Aboriginal people had been living in the Hobart area and all along the Derwent River for thousands of years before the British decided to create a settlement there. Many archaeological remains have been found throughout the Royal Tasmanian Botanical Gardens in Hobart. In particular, the shell middens reveal how significant this source of food was to the Muwinina's way of life.

HOBART'S COLONIAL HISTORY

Derwent River

Hobart is Australia's second oldest capital city. The British founded Hobart Town on the banks of the Derwent River in 1804, sixteen years after Sydney Town. At this time, Tasmania was called Van Diemen's Land and was part of the colony of New South Wales, under the jurisdiction of the Governor in Sydney Town.

The deep waters of the harbour at Hobart made it an ideal port for ships engaged in hunting whales and seals, two profitable industries in the early 1800s in Tasmania. The many coves and bays along the Derwent River encouraged the growth of shipbuilding, another early industry in Hobart. Before the invention of motor vehicles, trains and airplanes, ships were the fastest means of transport to the mainland and locations around Tasmania's coast.

Map of Van Diemen's Land

HOBART'S COLONIAL TIMELINE

01

1792
A French explorer discovered a large river on the southeast coast of Tasmania.

1793
John Hayes renamed the river discovered by the French, calling it the Derwent River.

1803
Governor King, the Governor of New South Wales and Van Diemen's Land, sent Lieutenant John Bowen to establish a convict settlement on the banks of the Derwent River. The aim was to discourage the French from taking possession of the island, and to create a place of punishment for the worst convicts from New South Wales.

04

1804
David Collins was appointed Lieutenant Governor of Van Diemen's Land. He relocated the previous settlement established by Bowen a year before. Moving it to Sullivans Cove, he established a town that eventually became Hobart.

1812
The first ship carrying convicts directly from England arrived.

1825
Van Diemen's Land became a separate colony.

1853
The last convict ship arrived in Hobart.

1856
The colony on Van Diemen's Land was renamed Tasmania.

1901
As a result of Federation, the state of Tasmania was created, with Hobart as its capital city.

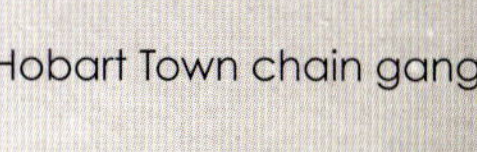
Hobart Town chain gang

Hobart Town Gazette, and VAN DIEMEN's LAND ADVERTISER.

PUBLISHED BY AUTHORITY.

VOL. VI.] SATURDAY, DECEMBER 1, 1821. [No. 291.

His Honor the Lieutenant Governor has thought proper to direct, that all Public Communications which may appear in the *Hobart Town Gazette, and Van Diemen's Land Advertiser*, ſigned with any Official Signature, are to be conſidered as Official Communcations made to thoſe Perſons to whom they may relate.

(By Command of His Honor) H. E. Robinson, *Secretary.*

HOBART TOWN GAZETTE.

The Sydney Gazette of the 10th ult. has been just received by the Messenger from Port Dalrymple; from which we copy the following intelligence of the arrival of His Excellency Major General Sir T. Brisbane, K. C. B. Lady Brisbane and Family, and His Excellency's Staff, at Port Jackson.

Under the Shipping Intelligence will be perceived the annunciation of the arrival from England, on Wedneſday laſt, of the merchant ſhip Royal George, Captain Powditch, on board of which veſſel has arrived His Excellency Major General Sir Thomas Brisbane, K. C. B. &c. &c. &c. with Lady Brisbane and infant Daughter, and Miſs M'Dougall, Siſter to Her Ladyſhip, together with His Excellency's Staff.

Upon the veſſel coming to an anchor in Sydney Cove, a ſalute of 19 guns was fired from Dawes' Battery; and immediately afterwards His Honor Lieutenant Governor Erskine proceeded on board, to pay his reſpects to His Excellency, and to greet Him on his ſafe arrival in New South Wales.—His Excellency was pleaſed to ſignify his intention of landing on the following morning.

On Thurſday morning, at ten o'clock, His Excellency left the Royal George, under the uſual ſalute due to his diſtinguiſhed rank, and landed at the private ſtairs on Bennelong's Point; where he was received by His Honor the Lieutenant Governor, and other Officers of the Colony; from whence he walked to Government-houſe, accompanied by Lady Brisbane, Family, and Staff; where Mrs. Macquarie, in the abſence of His Excellency Governor Macquarie, warmly welcomed Him, and Her Ladyſhip.—The full Band of His Majeſty's 48th Regiment paraded the lawn in front of Government-houſe, playing thoſe ſoothing and martial airs that tended to give a zeſt to that curioſity as well as ſenſibility naturally excited in the minds of all, upon ſo important and intereſting an occaſion. At the deſire (we believe) of His Excellency, the gates were thrown open, for the admiſſion of the Auſtralian Public, whoſe numbers quickly o'erſpread the walks around the domain, in order to catch a glimpſe of our future Governor—the Repreſentative of Our Gracious and Beloved Sovereign!—Carriages having been in readineſs, His Excellency and Family left the capital for Parramatta, in which town, we are given to underſtand, it is the deſign of His Excellency Sir Thomas Brisbane to reſide, during the abſence to the Northern Settlements of His Excellency Governor Macquarie, whoſe return to the Seat of Government we anticipate again to have the pleaſure of ſpeedily hailing.

Government and General Orders.

Government House, Hobart Town, Saturday, Nov. 24th, 1821.

THE Circumſtances and State of the Settlements of the Derwent, and of Port Dalrymple, having undergone eſſential Change ſince the Regulation was eſtabliſhed which required all Perſons, paſſing from one Settlement to the other, to have a Paſs, ſigned by the Lieutenant Governor or the Commandant; not only by the perfect State of Order and Tranquillity which has now for a long Period been eſtabliſhed in all Parts of the Country, but from the progreſſive Occupation and Settlement of the Interior of the Iſland, and the conſequent Approximation of the Settlements on the Southern and Northern Extremities:—It is notified, that the Regulation, which required all Perſons paſſing from one Settlement to the other to be provided with a Paſs, is aboliſhed, with Reſpect to Free Perſons.

But all the Regulations with Reſpect to Paſſes of Priſoners of the Crown remain in full Force; and in order to obviate any Riſk of Delay or Trouble which might ariſe to Free Perſons not known by thoſe whoſe Duty it is to examine Paſſes on the Road, it is recommended that, in traverſing the Country, they ſhould be provided with Means of ſhewing their Identity.

By Command of His Honor
The Lieutenant Governor,
H. E. Robinson, *Secretary.*

Government and General Orders.

Government House, Hobart Town, Saturday, November 24th, 1821.

THE Regulation, of Date February 20th, 1819, which requires the Name of the Owner, and his Place of Abode, and the Number of the Licenſe, to be painted upon all Carts worked on the Road within 10 Miles of Hobart Town, appearing not only to be much neglected, but to require more extended Application, it is now re-publiſhed for general Information and Guidance:—

"The increasing Number of Carts in Hobart Town and its Vicinity rendering it necessary for the Security of Persons and Property, that they should be Registered and Licensed, in Order to their being placed under Regulation according to Law;—

"*It is hereby ordered,* that on or before the 20th Day of March next, all Owners of Carts, Cars, and Timber Carriages in Hobart Town, or within Ten Miles thereof, shall take out a License at the Office of the Superintendant of Police. The Owner's Name, Number of Licenses and Place of Abode, shall be painted on the Outside of each Cart, Car, or Timber Carriage, in legible Letters and Figures; and any Owner neglecting to have his Cart, Car, or Timber Carriage so registered, licensed, and numbered, and his Name and Place of Abode so marked upon it, shall be subject to a Fine of not less than Twenty Shillings nor exceeding Five Pounds.

"Any Person driving a Cart, Car, or other Carriage, who shall leave it in the Streets or Road at such Distance that he cannot have proper Direction of the Cattle drawing the same; or who shall be found asleep therein; or who shall drive upon the Foot-paths; or who shall ride on such Cart or other Carriage, or on any of the Animals drawing it, unless with proper Reins for guiding them; or who shall by Negligence or wilful Misbehaviour cause Hurt or Damage to any Person or Carriage; or shall hinder or interrupt the free Passage of loaded Carts, Cars, or other Carriages, or of any Persons, on the Streets or Highway, shall, on Conviction, upon the View of a Magistrate, or otherwise before one or more Magistrates, be subject to a Fine of Ten Shillings, if such Driver be not the Owner, and if he be the Owner, to a Fine not exceeding Twenty Shillings; and in Default of Payment be committed to Gaol for any Period not exceeding one Month, unless the Fine be sooner Paid:—The Fine to go to the Party laying the Information."

And the Opening and Formation of Roads in different Parts of the Country by Government having been effected, and being in Progreſs, to a conſiderable Extent, and the Number of Wheel Carriages and the Traffic on theſe Roads being greatly increaſed ſince the Promulgation of the above Regulation;—It is hereby ordered and directed, that the Regulation of the 20th February, 1819, ſhall, in its ſeveral Proviſions, apply to all Carts and other Deſcription of Carriage therein ſpecified, throughout the Settlements in Van Diemen's Land:—thoſe in the County of Buckinghamſhire to be Licenſed as before ordered by the Superintendant of Police at Hobart Town, and thoſe of the County of Cornwall by the Magiſtrates of that County; and all Owners of ſuch Carriages will take Notice, that the Names, Place of Abode, and Number of Licenſe, are to be painted and not marked in Chalk, or any Subſtance liable to be rubbed off.

The ſaid Extenſion of this Regulation to all Carts in Van Diemen's Land, to take Place from the 1ſt January, 1822.

By Command of His Honor
The Lieutenant Governor,
H. E. Robinson, *Secretary.*

Government and General Orders.

Government House, Hobart Town, December, 1st, 1821.

DENNIS SULLIVAN is appointed a Conſtable for Hobart Town.

By Command of His Honor
The Lieutenant Governor,
H. E. Robinson, Secretary.

CROWN DEBTS.

Commiſſariat Office, Hobart Town, Nov. 17th, 1821.

NOTICE.—Perſons indebted to Government are again informed, that the Stores here and at Port Dalrymple will continue Open during this and the following Month, for the Reception of Wheat or Meat in Liquidation of ſaid Debts;—When, conformably with Orders received, a Statement of thoſe outſtanding will be tranſmitted to Sydney.

A Liſt of Promiſſory Notes for Merino Rams, remaining unpaid, will be publiſhed in the firſt Gazette in January. A. Moodie, *A. C. G.*

Commiſſariat Office, Hobart Town, Nov. 24th, 1821

TENDERS to Supply His Majeſty's Stores in Van Diemen's Land with FRESH MEAT, for the Quarter commencing 25th December next, muſt be tranſmitted to me here, and to Deputy Aſſiſtant Commiſſary General Roberts at George Town, on or before the 10th of that Month.

☞ Printed Forms of Tenders to be had at the reſpective Offices. A. Moodie, *A. C. G.*

HOBART'S NEWSPAPERS

The Hobart Town Gazette was one of the earliest newspapers in Australia. Its first issue appeared in 1816, twelve years after Hobart was established. It initially included both government notices as well as general news. *The Hobart Town Gazette* is a wonderful primary resource for anyone who wants to find out for themselves what was happening day by day in early Hobart.

SATURDAY, DECEMBER 1, 1821

"Mr. E. Hobson ... proposes to open in Hobart Town, about Christmas, a Grammar School, in which will be taught the Greek, Latin, French, and English languages; arithmetic and merchants' accounts; geography and the use of the globes; those branches of the mathematics and natural philosophy that are usually entered upon in the schools of the mother country, comprising mensuration of solids, surfaces, heights, and distances; land surveying, geometry, algebra, trigonemetry, and navigation; together with the doctrine of fluxions, and the principles of mechanics, optics, hydrostatics, etc. Terms - fifteen guineas a year."

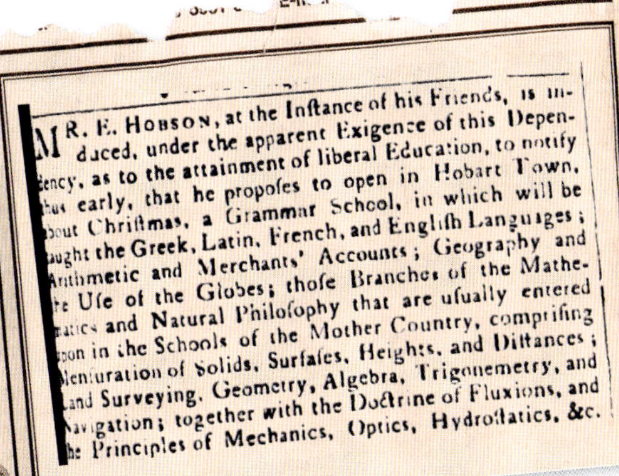

MR. E. HOBSON, at the Inftance of his Friends, is induced, under the apparent Exigence of this Depen-
ency, as to the attainment of liberal Education, to notify
hus early, that he propofes to open in Hobart Town,
bout Chriftmas, a Grammar School, in which will be
ught the Greek, Latin, French, and Englifh Languages;
rithmetic and Merchants' Accounts; Geography and
e Ufe of the Globes; thofe Branches of the Mathe-
atics and Natural Philofophy that are ufually entered
pon in the Schools of the Mother Country, comprifing
lenfuration of Solids, Surfaces, Heights, and Diftances;
and Surveying, Geometry, Algebra, Trigonemetry, and
avigation; together with the Doctrine of Fluxions, and
he Principles of Mechanics, Optics, Hydroftatics, &c.

Children at a private school in early Hobart were expected to learn many STEM subjects.

Notice the different ways people used to spell and punctuate compared with the rules we use today.

Can you see the 'f' used instead of an 's'?

The Mercury

The Mercury newspaper first appeared in the 1850s and is still published in Hobart.

Hobart Mercury building

DERWENT RIVER

The Derwent River begins at Lake St Clair in the centre of Tasmania. It flows through Hobart before entering the sea at Storm Bay. The river estuary provided a safe harbour for sailing ships, and this was a reason for locating Hobart Town on its banks in 1804.

Before the end of the last Ice Age, when the sea level was much lower than today, the Derwent River extended along a course that is now covered by sea, and its prehistoric riverbanks are now deep under the water.

The Derwent River suffered from pollution during the 20th century, but the cleaner waters today have attracted whales and dolphins back into its sheltered bays.

Sydney Hobart Yacht Race

The annual Sydney Hobart Yacht Race begins in Sydney Harbour and ends on the Derwent River in Hobart. Beginning on Boxing Day, the sailors race their yachts down the east coast of Australia, covering a distance of 628 nautical miles. The finishing line is at Battery Point in Hobart.

DERWENT ESTUARY

The Derwent Estuary extends from the town of New Norfolk down to South Arm. It is an area where the tidal flow of seawater moves upstream and mixes with the freshwater flowing down towards the sea. The estuary is a habitat for many aquatic animals. They share the waterway with people who use the river for transport, fishing and recreation.

Parts of the Derwent Estuary are marine reserves and wildlife sanctuaries. The habitats for wildlife are varied and support many species of plants and animals.

Little Pied Cormorants

Derwent Estuary Wildlife Habitats

- Saltmarsh
- Tidal flats
- Wetlands
- Reefs
- Seagrass beds
- Beaches
- Inter-tidal zones

Beaches

The Derwent Estuary is bordered by many beaches. Although the winter months are too cold for swimming, people in Hobart enjoy their easy access to these areas for swimming and water sports during the summer.

COAL RIVER

The colonists who founded Hobart soon spread out to explore and claim more land. Just north of Hobart and the Derwent River is the Coal River. Its valley offered fertile land for farming and pastures for cattle. There was also coal under the ground for mining.

While farmers had been living in the area for many years, the colonists officially named the new town of Richmond in 1824.

The Richmond Bridge, completed in 1825 and built using convict labour, is now one of Australia's historic treasures. It is the oldest bridge still in use anywhere in Australia.

Richmond Bridge

Chequered Blue Butterfly

Ramsar Wetlands

The Coal River opens out into an area called Pitt Water, an internationally recognised wetlands region. Along with the Orielton Lagoon, Pitt Water was declared a Ramsar Site in 1994. Ramsar is an organisation which aims to list wetlands around the world and encourage their preservation. The Pitt Water - Orielton Lagoon wetlands close to Hobart are a vital resting location for birds which migrate all the way from the Arctic in the northern hemisphere. The wetlands are also a habitat for the very rare chequered blue butterfly. The nearby Woody Island and Barren Island are located towards the mouth of the Coal River. They are also important wildlife sites used by migrating birds.

MOUNT WELLINGTON

With an elevation of 1,271 metres, Mount Wellington is the highest point near Hobart, which sits on its foothills. Wellington Park is easily accessible from Hobart, and has mountain forest areas right on the city's doorstep. A lookout at the top of Mount Wellington provides extensive views across Hobart below.

Organ Pipes

Created when molten rock came to the surface many millions of years ago, Mount Wellington still has features left from those ancient times. The Organ Pipes are a group of dolerite columns that formed when magma rose to the surface and hardened into rocks that look like huge pipes.

European explorers gave the mountain many different names, but the British finally settled on naming it after the Duke of Wellington, who defeated Napoleon in the famous Battle of Waterloo in 1815. The mountain is now officially known by its dual Aboriginal and English name of kunanyi / Mount Wellington.

Charles Darwin 1880

Charles Darwin climbed Mount Wellington when he visited Hobart in 1836, marvelling at the forests and the views, just as tourists do today. Darwin had to find his own way through the bush, but visitors now enjoy a much easier climb, using tracks or the road to reach the summit. Darwin's scientific work is the basis of the modern study of the evolution of plants and animals on Earth.

THE ANTARCTIC

Antarctic Exploration

Hobart has been a departure point for the great Antarctic explorers since the early 20th century. In 1911, Roald Amundsen led the first expedition to reach the South Pole. He then journeyed to Hobart to announce his achievement to the world, using the local telegraph service.

Douglas Mawson left from Hobart on his expedition of 1911 to 1914, during which he mapped the Antarctic coastline and performed scientific investigations.

The Mawson's Huts Replica Museum in Hobart is a reconstruction of the accommodation that Mawson and his team used during their heroic but ill-fated Australian Antarctic Expedition.

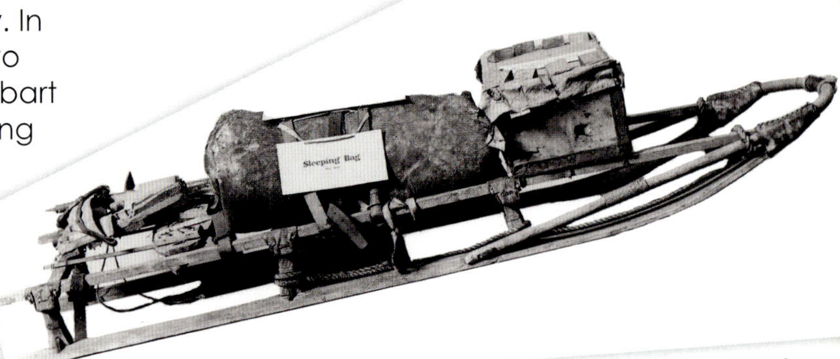

Mawson's sledge

Tasmanian Polar Network

The Tasmanian Polar Network is a group of businesses, research organisations and government agencies that are all focussed on exploration and research in the Antarctic and Southern Ocean.

These services are not only provided for Australian operations. Many other countries that visit the Antarctic use Hobart as their base, making use of the technical expertise and essential supplies that Hobart offers.

Some of the products and services of the TPN include:

- providing scientific equipment
- installing equipment in specialised vessels
- providing food supplies for expeditions
- managing waste for expeditions

ANIMAL PESTS IN HOBART

Authorities in Tasmania undertake strict biosecurity procedures to keep Tasmania free of imported pests and weeds. The Port of Hobart receives shipping from around the world, and all of these vessels are potential sources of unwanted plant and animal life.

Foxes were imported into Tasmania in the 1800s on purpose for the sport of hunting, but today Tasmania aims to be free of this pest animal. Although there are no foxes known to be in Tasmania at present, this situation could easily change if a pregnant fox manages to stowaway on a ship from the Australian mainland and escapes when the ship arrives.

Pest animals already in Hobart include:

- Trout
- European wasps
- European bumblebees
- European honey bees
- Feral cats
- Feral goats
- Rabbits

HOBART'S NATIVE WILDLIFE

The Last Tasmanian Tiger

The Beaumaris Zoo in Hobart closed many years ago, but it was the place where the very last Tasmanian Tiger died in 1936. Hunted to extinction, the Tasmanian Tiger was once considered a dangerous livestock predator that had to be destroyed. Today, scientists are working on research into DNA technology that could bring the Tasmanian Tiger back to life through cloning. Parts of the Tasmanian wilderness are very remote, and people occasionally think they have seen a Tasmanian Tiger roaming through the forests.

Tasmanian Devils

In the early 1800s, there were so many Tasmanian Devils around the settlement at Hobart that rewards were offered for people who killed them. The Devils attacked chickens and lambs and were a nuisance to the farmers.
In 1941, Devils became a protected species, but their numbers continue to fall due to an infectious and deadly facial cancer. The best place to see Tasmanian Devils in Hobart is at a wildlife sanctuary.

Native Wildlife in Greater Hobart

Hobart is close to many areas of natural forest that provide safe habitats for native wildlife. Here are just a few of the native animals that live on the fringes of human settlement on land and in the water near Hobart:

- Bandicoots
- Black Cockatoos
- Dolphins
- Humpback Whales
- Little Penguins
- Pademelons
- Platypuses
- Rosellas
- Southern Right Whales
- White Cockatoos
- Wombats

Native Animals That Hibernate

Hibernation is an adaptation that allows animals to survive harsh winter conditions. They just sleep right through the coldest seasons! The word hibernation comes from a Latin word meaning 'to pass the winter'.

Most of Australia is too warm for animals to need to hibernate. They will not freeze and they can still find food in the winter. In parts of Tasmania, the winters are so cold that a form of hibernation is the only option for some animals to survive. They go into a state called torpor. This is like hibernation but it does not usually last as long as it does for animals living in colder parts of the world.

Eastern Pygmy Possum

Animals that experience torpor or hibernation in Tasmania:

Long-Eared Bats

Pygmy Possums

Snakes

Echidnas

International Wildlife Agreements

Australia has signed agreements with other nations to protect migratory birds and their local habitats, some of which are very close to Hobart.

- Republic of Korea-Australia Migratory Bird Agreement
- China-Australia Migratory Bird Agreement
- Japan-Australia Migratory Bird Agreement

Shy Albatross

HOBART'S PEOPLE

35,000 years ago

Ancestors of the Aboriginal people journeyed into Tasmania when it was joined to the rest of Australia by dry land.

1804

Hobart Town's population included convicts and marines as guards.

03

1853

The last convict ship arrived in Hobart. Without the labour that the convicts provided, Hobart's development was slow. The Gold Rush of the mid 1800s further reduced the working population of the town as men left to seek their fortunes on the goldfields.

Convict ship Mount Stuart Elphinstone

The Australian census of 2016 revealed many interesting facts about Greater Hobart

Growth

Hobart experienced the lowest population growth in the ten years to 2016 of any capital city across Australia. While the national increase in population was 18% over that period, Hobart's population increased by only about 10%.

Hobart has a much higher proportion of people born in Australia amongst its population than does the rest of Australia.

	Hobart	Rest of Australia
Born in Australia	80%	67%

Top countries of birth for people in Greater Hobart

01 Australia
02 England
03 China
04 New Zealand
05 India
06 Germany

Royal Hobart Hospital

Workers

About 44% of all the people employed across Tasmania work in Greater Hobart. Most of them work in health care, social welfare, shops and construction.

HOBART AND GOVERNMENT

Timeline of Government in Tasmania

Before Colonisation
Tasmanian Aboriginal nations governed according to their own laws.

Until 1825
Van Diemen's Land was administered from Sydney.

1825
Van Diemen's Land became a separate colony.

1856
The colony was renamed Tasmania and its government met for the first time.

1901
Federation meant that Tasmania became a state of Australia.

1904
Women were allowed to vote in Tasmania.

1922
Women were allowed to stand for election to parliament in Tasmania.

Parliament House

Parliament House in Hobart was designed by John Lee Archer, not as a home for the government, but as a Customs House. The Derwent River originally ran much closer to the building than it does today, making it easy for customs officials to inspect the cargo on ships. Sandstone for the construction was quarried nearby, and a small railway was built to carry the heavy blocks to the building site. Customs House was altered to accommodate the first colonial parliament in 1856, and it has been Tasmania's Parliament House ever since.

Government House

Government House was built in 1857 and was designed by William Porden Kay. It is an example of a Victorian era country house and is one of the largest of its style in Australia. The building replaced the previous Government House which was constructed in Macquarie Street, Hobart, in 1817.

HOBART CITY COUNCIL

Hobart gained its own elected town council in 1853. The first Mayor was William Carter.

Hobart Town Hall

Hobart Town Hall dates from the 1860s. It was designed by architect Henry Hunter, who was also responsible for many other notable buildings around Hobart.

Tram in Macquarie Street

Sister cities

Yaizu, Japan and L'Aquila, Italy

Friendship City Agreements

Xi'an and Fuzhou in China.

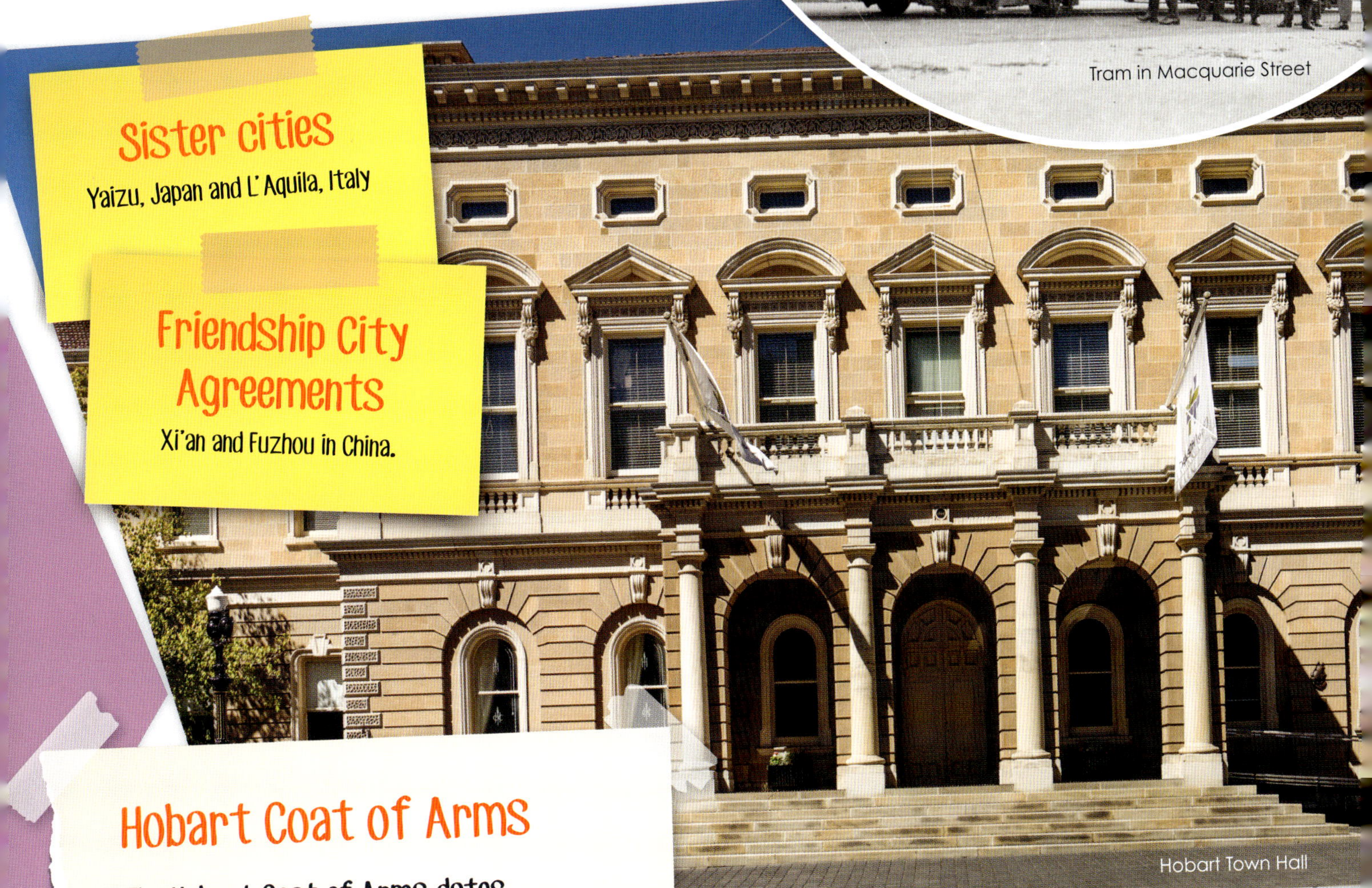

Hobart Town Hall

Hobart Coat of Arms

The Hobart Coat of Arms dates from 1953.

Motto - Thus in strength did Hobart grow

Animals - Tasmanian Emu and the Forester Kangaroo, both wearing collars of apples

HOBART'S ESSENTIAL SERVICES

Water

Although Hobart was founded on the banks of the Derwent River, the water from the river near Hobart is salty and not suitable for drinking or for watering crops. Small streams, mostly with sources in Mount Wellington, provided the first colonists with their water supply. The early settlement at Risdon Cove had to be moved to the present site of Hobart in 1804 because there was no fresh water available. The growing population soon needed more water than was supplied by small streams, so dams were built on water sources flowing from Mount Wellington. Dams were also needed on the parts of the Derwent River that were not affected by seawater flowing into them from the estuary.

Derwert River

Hydroelectricity

Hobart has had power supplied by hydroelectricity since the state government completed the first hydroelectric power station in 1916. Hydroelectricity uses the power of swift flowing water to turn large turbines that generate electricity. During droughts, when the water supply to hydroelectricity plants decreases, Tasmania also uses gas to generate power. In contrast with large parts of the Australian mainland, Tasmania does not have any local coal-fired plants to generate electricity. Wind farms supply a small proportion of Hobart's electricity needs.

Basslink is an undersea connection that can transmit electricity between Tasmania and the Australian mainland. Via Basslink, Tasmanians can access power generated on the mainland, or they can send power back along Basslink to other states that are part of the shared network.

Waddamana, Hobart's first hydropower station

Sewerage

In the early days of settlement, raw sewage was dumped straight into the Derwent River. This is no longer the case, and sewage from homes and businesses in Hobart is now processed in Sewage Treatment Plants.

TRANSPORT IN HOBART

Horse-Drawn Coaches

The first horse-drawn coach service began in Tasmania in the late 1820s. Coach services were expensive and the poor roads made them very uncomfortable.

Railways and Buses

Hobart does not have any passenger trains as they stopped running in 1978. TasRail operates freight services to link some towns to each other and to ports. Buses are the main form of public transport.

Trams

The first tram began operating in Hobart in 1893. Trams ceased running in 1960, when buses and motor cars became a more popular means of transport.

Ferries

Ferry services operated across the Derwent River from the times of the early settlement of Hobart. The eventual construction of bridges across the river made most of these ferry services unnecessary.

Constitution Dock, Hobart

Port of Hobart

There are four major ports in Tasmania, with the Port of Hobart being one of them. This port is a location for international export and import by shipping. It also provides berths for cruise ships that visit Hobart.

Hobart was once Tasmania's main port city, used by whaling ships and exporters of the state's timber and wool. Ports on the northern coast of Tasmania gradually took some of this business away from Hobart. Being closer to the Australian mainland and to other destinations beyond Australia, the journeys from the northern ports were faster.

BUSINESS AND INDUSTRY IN HOBART

Agriculture

Outside the city centre of Hobart, large areas are devoted to livestock grazing and nature conservation. Across all of Greater Hobart, over 40% of the land is used for agriculture. Fruits and vegetables grown in Greater Hobart, and across the rest of Tasmania, have a reputation for being 'clean and green'.

Tasmanian Polar Network

The Tasmanian Polar Network, TPN, is based in Hobart. It provides services for Antarctic research and tourism vessels.

Tourism

Tourism is a major contributor to Hobart's economy. In 2016, 900,000 people visited Hobart, spending money on services and creating local employment opportunities. About another 140,000 visitors arrived on cruise ships to enjoy a stay in Hobart.

Commercial Fishing

Hobart is Tasmania's main fishing port for commercial fishing vessels. As well as providing a variety of wild seafood for Australia and for export, Hobart is also known for its salmon farming industry.

Wineglass Bay

PLACES TO SEE IN HOBART

Battery Point

- Battery Point
- Cascades Female Factory
- Maritime Museum of Tasmania
- Mawson's Huts
- MONA (Museum of Old and New Art)
- kunanyi / Mount Wellington
- Salamanca Market
- Tasmanian Museum and Art Gallery

Mount Wellington

MONA (Museum of Old and New Art)

- Hobart Synagogue
- Narryna Heritage Museum
- Parliament House
- Royal Tasmanian Botanical Gardens
- Tasmanian Transport Museum
- Wrest Point Casino

Cascades Female Factory

HOBART'S UNESCO WORLD HERITAGE SITE

In the colonial era, female factories were places where women convicts lived and worked. They did sewing, washing, cleaning and other work considered suitable for women at the time. The factory was a prison, a home, a place where convicts' children were housed until they were sent to orphanages, and a place of reform, where women supposedly learned work skills. The Cascades Female Factory housed women prisoners from 1828 to 1877.

The Cascades Female Factory is one of the most interesting buildings from Australia's colonial past. It is now a UNESCO World Heritage Site, with international significance because of the insight the surroundings give into the way female convicts were treated in the past.

Arthur Circus

Battery Point

Battery Point is an area of Hobart where the Georgian history of Tasmania comes alive. The historic buildings and sites are a reminder of Hobart's past, when rows of cannons that faced the water gave the place its name. The cannons were put in place in the early 1800s to repel any invasion by ships from other nations.

Arthur Circus, in Battery Point, is a circular street with cottages surrounding a private park. It is a rare survivor in Australia of a colonial style of townscape.

Salamanca Market

The Salamanca Market began as a small community market in 1972 and has now grown to become a tourist attraction. In the early 1800s, the original markets for the town of Hobart were also located beside the Derwent River, not far from the modern Salamanca Market.

Wrest Point Casino

Wrest Point Casino, the first legal casino in Australia, was opened at Sandy Bay in 1973. For some years it was the only legal casino in Australia.

Greater Hobart Trails

There are many opportunities for walkers to explore the city of Hobart and its natural surroundings. The Greater Hobart Trails project offers people the opportunity to find historic sites, bushland and waterfalls, all within or not far from the city centre. The trails have a mix of terrains allowing walking, cycling, horse riding and mountain bike riding.

Hobart Synagogue

Australia's oldest synagogue still being used is located in Hobart. Built in a style of architecture called Egyptian revival, the synagogue dates from 1845. The Hobart synagogue is unusual in having a section that was set aside for Jewish convicts who were allowed to attend prayers there.

Salamanca Market

Walking trail, Mount Wellington

GLOSSARY

DNA	genetic material in living things
cloning	creating a new individual through DNA technology
dolerite	type of rock formed from magma
magma	molten rock beneath the surface of the Earth
foothills	hills below the top of a mountain
estuary	part of a river where it enters the sea
intertidal zone	place on land between high and low tides
to exile	to force a person to leave their country
archaeology	study of the remains from human history
nautical mile	unit of measurement used at sea
biosecurity	providing protection from pests and biological hazards
to stowaway	to hide in a ship that is leaving port